GOOD HEARTY SOUPS

By Karen Plageman

Illustrated by Dennis Redmond

Library of Congress
Catalogue Number 78-70972

ISBN 0-915942-12-7

First Printing, December, 1978

Editor: Susan Herbert

OWLSWOOD PRODUCTIONS COOKBOOKS:
BUNDT CAKES by Karen Plageman and Susan Herbert
THE WOK WAY by Winnie Tuan
SLOW-CROCK COOKERY by Karen Plageman
THE CRÊPE BOOK by Susan Herbert
BRAVO! ITALIAN COOKING by Cynthia Scheer
BAKE BREAD by Marguerite Bencivenga and Barbara Brauer
FRENCH COUNTRY FAVORITES by Cynthia Scheer
NATURAL FIBER COOKING by Karen Plageman
GERMAN HOME COOKING by Cynthia Scheer
THE FOOD PROCESSOR BOOK by Pam Biele and Susan Walter
THE MICROWAVE WAY by Dorothy McNett
MEXICAN COOKING by Cynthia Scheer
GOOD HEARTY SOUPS by Karen Plageman

TABLE OF CONTENTS

ABOUT THE AUTHOR

GOOD, HEARTY SOUPS is Karen Plageman's fourth cookbook for Owlswood Productions. In 1973, Ms. Plageman co-authored BUNDT CAKES, and in 1974 was the first in the United States with a cookbook for the electric slow cooker, SLOW-CROCK COOKERY. Her third book, NATURAL FIBER COOKING, like GOOD HEARTY SOUPS, features wholesome, family oriented recipes.

Ms. Plageman received her degree in Home Economics from Florida State University. Later, she travelled and lived abroad, gaining firsthand experience of varied Continental cuisines. She has taught a variety of cooking classes, from baking to Chinese wok cooking. At present, Ms. Plageman devotes her time to recipe research and development, and serves as a Home Economics Advisor for Owlswood Productions.

Karen Plageman, her husband and their three children live in the San Francisco Bay Area.

INTRODUCTION

What can be better than a kettle of homemade soup simmering on the stove? Fresh, hand-picked vegetables, meats, seafoods, seasoned in a hearty broth?

GOOD HEARTY SOUPS is a special collection of soup recipes, each of which is a main dish in itself. Whether with sandwiches or salad for a family supper, or with crackers for a quick, satisfying lunch, soup is always a refreshing favorite. Just add your favorite complements—soup goes great with almost everything. And, because all the vitamins and minerals of the ingredients are cooked right into the soup without waste, soup is an economical and nutritious meal.

Here are soups for every taste and every season: rich, creamy soups for a chilly winter's evening, vegetarian soups with garden fresh flavor, delicious seafood soups and exciting chicken and meat soups to satisfy the biggest appetites.

Preparing soups couldn't be easier! Each one will be just as good as the wholesome ingredients you add. Feel free to experiment with recipes: add your own favorite vegetables or spices, adjust the seasonings to your family's preference. Or, combine two leftover soups to make a whole new soup.

Soups don't have to take a long time to prepare. Some recipes in GOOD HEARTY SOUPS take only an hour or less from start to finish.

STOCKS: Most soups begin with stock or broth. This is the liquid in which meat or vegetables have been simmered to bring out all the flavor and nutrition for your soup. In GOOD HEARTY SOUPS there are three basic stocks: beef, vegetable and chicken. You can prepare the stock a day ahead to have on hand when you are ready to begin your soup. (Use fresh stock within 3 to 5 days after making it.) Or, you can freeze stock in convenient quantities for use later on.

While homemade stocks are best, both canned broths and bouillon cubes may be substituted with good results. Canned broths come in both concentrated and regular-strength varieties. Read the label to find cooking instructions. When using bouillon cubes instead of stock, omit the salt in the recipe.

FREEZING: All soups and stocks may be successfully frozen, retaining their flavors for 3 to 6 months. Make sure to use freezer-proof containers (check glass containers especially). Leave enough room at the top for expansion. Many manufacturers provide a freezing line for this purpose.

SOUP BONES AND MEAT: When buying bones for stock or soups, select meaty ones. Inexpensive cuts of meat are best in soups since they provide more flavor and are quite tender after simmering.

VEGETABLES: FROZEN OR FRESH? Many recipes in GOOD HEARTY SOUPS indicate when frozen vegetables may be used in place of fresh vegetables. However, because soup making is so flexible, frozen vegetables may always be substituted for fresh vegetables with good results.

SERVING AMOUNTS: The recipes in GOOD HEARTY SOUPS indicate the quantity of soup yielded in quarts, not servings. Of course appetites vary, but you may use these guidelines. When serving soup as a first course, plan on 1 cup of soup per person. When the soup will be the main dish, plan on 1-1/2 to 2 cups per person.

START WITH A BASIC STOCK

BASIC BEEF STOCK*
an excellent basis for your favorite soups

6 pounds beef neck bones or an equal amount of
  leftover beef bones and scraps, such as from a roast
1 extra large onion, quartered
2 large carrots
4 ribs of celery

4 sprigs of parsley
1/4 teaspoon thyme
1 tablespoon salt
6 quarts (24 cups) water

In a large kettle, combine beef neck bones, onion, carrots, celery, parsley, thyme, salt and water. Bring to a boil, reduce heat, cover and simmer for 4 to 4-1/2 hours. Remove beef neck bones and save any meat for other uses. Strain stock and refrigerate overnight. Discard layer of fat that has collected on top of stock. Freeze or refrigerate until ready to use. (If refrigerated, use stock within 3 to 5 days.) Makes 4 quarts.

*Please note that canned beef broth or beef bouillon cubes may be successfully substituted for Basic Beef Stock. Follow manufacturer's directions. (Important: if substituting bouillon cubes, omit salt in the recipe.)

BASIC CHICKEN STOCK*
a flavorful base for any number of soups

4 pounds chicken backs, necks or wings or an equal amount of leftover
   chicken bones and scraps, such as a chicken carcass
3 quarts (12 cups) water
1 large onion, quartered
2 large ribs of celery
1 large carrot
2 teaspoons salt

In a large kettle, combine chicken pieces, water, onion, celery, carrot and salt. Bring to a boil, reduce heat, cover and simmer for 2 to 2-1/2 hours. Remove bones and save any meat for other uses. Strain stock and refrigerate overnight. Discard layer of fat that has collected on the surface. Refrigerate or freeze until ready to use. (If refrigerated, use stock within 3 to 5 days.) Makes 3 quarts.

*Please note that canned chicken broth or chicken bouillon cubes may be successfully substituted for Basic Chicken Stock. Follow manufacturer's directions. (Important: if substituting bouillon cubes, omit salt in the recipe.)

BASIC VEGETABLE STOCK*
a soup foundation full of vitamins and minerals

3 or 4 medium-size ribs of celery, quartered
4 medium-size carrots, quartered
1 head (about 4 cups) romaine lettuce, quartered
3 cups chopped, fresh parsley
3 or 4 medium-size turnips *or* 1 large rutabaga,
   quartered
1 extra large onion, quartered

4 whole cloves
1 large bay leaf
1/2 teaspoon savory
1/2 teaspoon thyme
1 tablespoon salt
5 quarts (20 cups) water

In a large kettle, combine celery, carrots, romaine lettuce, parsley, turnips, onion, cloves, bay leaf, savory, thyme, salt and water. Bring to a boil, reduce heat, cover and simmer for 2 hours. Strain and discard vegetables. Freeze or refrigerate stock until ready to use. (If refrigerated, use within 3 to 5 days.) Makes 4 quarts.

*Please note that vegetable bouillon cubes may be successfully substituted for Basic Vegetable Stock. When substituting, omit the salt in the recipe.

A GARDEN VARIETY OF VEGETABLE SOUPS

TOMATO ZUCCHINI SOUP
a delicious way to use that plentiful zucchini

1/4 cup butter or margarine
1-1/2 cups chopped onions
1-1/2 quarts (6 cups) basic chicken *or*
  basic vegetable stock (see pages 8, 9)
2 (28 oz.) cans tomatoes and their liquid
1 tablespoon salt
1/4 teaspoon lemon pepper
1/2 teaspoon basil

1/2 teaspoon paprika
1/4 teaspoon mace
1 bay leaf
4 whole cloves
1/2 cup white rice
2 cups thinly sliced celery
1 pound zucchini, thinly sliced

In a large kettle, melt butter or margarine and sauté onions until they are barely golden brown. Add chicken or vegetable stock, tomatoes, their liquid, salt, lemon pepper, basil, paprika, mace, bay leaf and whole cloves; bring to a boil. Reduce heat and simmer, covered, for 45 minutes. Remove from heat; discard bay leaf and cloves. In an electric blender or food processor, whirl soup (two to three cups at a time) until smooth. Return soup to kettle; add rice and simmer 15 minutes, stirring several times. Add celery and zucchini; continue to simmer an additional 10 minutes or until vegetables are still slightly crisp. Makes 3-1/2 quarts.

GARDEN VEGETABLE SOUP
this meatless soup is both refreshing and filling

2 cups chopped onions
1 cup sliced celery and leaves
3 cloves garlic, minced
2 tablespoons butter or margarine
2 quarts (8 cups) water
1 (16 oz.) can tomato purée
1-1/2 teaspoons salt
1/4 teaspoon pepper
1/2 teaspoon savory
1/2 teaspoon dill weed
1/2 teaspoon mace

1/2 cup chopped fresh parsley
1 cup chopped carrots
2 cups fresh lima beans *or*
   1 (10 oz.) package frozen lima beans
2 cups cubed yellow crookneck squash *or*
   1 (10 oz.) package frozen crookneck squash
2 cups small cauliflower pieces *or*
   1 (10 oz.) package frozen cauliflower
2 cups fresh green peas *or*
   1 (10 oz.) package frozen green peas

In a large kettle, sauté the onions, celery and garlic in butter or margarine until onions are limp. Add the water, tomato purée, salt, pepper, savory, dill weed, mace, parsley, carrots and lima beans; bring to a boil. Reduce heat and simmer, covered, for 30 minutes. Add squash and cauliflower; continue to simmer another 20 minutes. Add peas and simmer an additional 10 minutes. Makes 4 quarts.

BROCCOLI SOUP
this captures all the flavorful goodness of broccoli

1-1/2 cups chopped onions
1-1/3 cups chopped celery and leaves
1/3 cup chopped fresh parsley
3 cloves garlic, minced
2 quarts (8 cups) basic chicken *or*
   basic vegetable stock (see pages 8, 9)
4 cups chopped, fresh broccoli *or*
   2 (10 oz.) packages frozen, chopped broccoli

2-1/2 cups diced potatoes
1 teaspoon salt
1/8 teaspoon pepper
1/4 teaspoon thyme
1/4 teaspoon marjoram
1/4 teaspoon rosemary
1/4 teaspoon nutmeg

In a large kettle, combine onions, celery, parsley, garlic, chicken or vegetable stock, broccoli, potatoes, salt, pepper and seasonings. Bring to a boil, reduce heat and simmer, covered, for 30 minutes. Remove 2 to 3 cups of soup and purée in a food processor, electric blender, or by forcing through a strainer. Return puréed soup to kettle and stir to mix well. Reheat soup to serving temperature. Makes 3 quarts.

SUPPER CHOWDER
perfect to serve at a late evening supper

4 cups cubed potatoes
1-1/2 cups chopped onions
1-1/2 cups chopped celery and leaves
1 tablespoon salt
1 quart (4 cups) water
1/2 cup butter or margarine
1/2 cup all-purpose flour

2 teaspoons salt
1/4 teaspoon pepper
2 teaspoons dry mustard
1 quart (4 cups) milk
3-1/2 cups shredded sharp cheddar cheese
2 tablespoons parsley flakes
1 (28 oz.) can stewed tomatoes and their liquid

In a large kettle, combine potatoes, onions, celery, salt and water; bring to a boil. Reduce heat and simmer, uncovered, for 15 minutes or until potatoes are tender. In a medium size pot, melt butter or margarine; add flour, salt, pepper and mustard, stirring to make a smooth paste. Gradually stir in milk; cook over medium heat until bubbly, stirring constantly. Add cheese and stir until melted. Pour cheese sauce into potato mixture and mix well. Add parsley flakes, stewed tomatoes and their liquid; stir and continue to cook over low heat until hot enough to serve. Makes 4 quarts.

13

SWISS CHARD SOUP
high in fiber—with lentils, brown rice and cracked wheat

1-1/2 pounds Swiss chard
1/2 cup dried lentils
1/3 cup brown rice
1/4 cup cracked wheat
1 cup chopped onions
4 cloves garlic, minced
2 quarts (8 cups) basic vegetable stock (see page 9)
1 quart (4 cups) water
1 (15 oz.) can tomato sauce
2 teaspoons salt
1/2 teaspoon pepper

Wash chard thoroughly and drain. Separate the thick, white stalks and the leaves. Coarsely chop stalks and set aside. Chop leaves and set aside in another container. In a large kettle, combine the lentils, brown rice, cracked wheat, onions, garlic, vegetable stock, water, tomato sauce, salt and pepper. Bring to a boil, reduce heat and simmer, covered, for 30 minutes. Add coarsely chopped chard stalks and continue to simmer, covered, another 45 minutes. Finally, add chopped chard leaves and simmer, covered, an additional 15 minutes. Makes 4 quarts.

VEGETARIAN VEGETABLE SOUP
exceptionally full-bodied and nutritious

3 to 5 leeks, well rinsed and sliced thin (about 2 cups)
1-1/2 cups sliced carrots
1-1/2 cups sliced celery
1 cup diced potatoes
1/2 cup pearl barley
2 quarts (8 cups) basic vegetable stock
   (see page 9)
1 (28 oz.) can tomatoes, chopped, and their liquid
1 cup water
2 cups fresh cut green beans *or*
   1 (10 oz.) package frozen cut green beans
2 cups chopped escarole *or*
   1 (10 oz.) package frozen escarole
1 teaspoon salt
1/4 teaspoon pepper

In a large kettle, combine the leeks, carrots, celery, potatoes, barley, vegetable stock, tomatoes, their liquid and water. Bring to a boil, reduce heat and simmer, covered, for 1 hour. Add green beans, escarole, salt and pepper. Continue to simmer, covered, for another 30 minutes. Makes 4 quarts.

BASIL BEAN SOUP
sprinkle each serving with Parmesan cheese and chopped parsley

1/2 pound dried, white kidney beans, *soaked overnight in 4 cups water*
1-1/2 quarts (6 cups) water
1 (16 oz.) can tomatoes, chopped, and their liquid
1-1/2 cups chopped onions
1 cup chopped celery
1 cup chopped carrots
1 cup chopped potatoes

1 cup chopped turnips
1 tablespoon salt
1/4 teaspoon crushed, dried red peppers
1 bay leaf
1 tablespoon basil leaves
1 pound zucchini, chopped
1/2 cup dry sherry *or* dry white wine
grated Parmesan cheese and fresh parsley for garnish

In a large kettle, combine the white kidney beans, their soaking liquid, water, tomatoes and their liquid, onions, celery, carrots, potatoes, turnips, salt, red pepper, bay leaf and basil. Bring to a boil; reduce heat and simmer, covered, for 1-1/2 hours or until beans are tender. Add zucchini and sherry; continue to simmer for 20 minutes. Sprinkle each serving with grated Parmesan cheese and garnish with chopped parsley. Makes 4 quarts.

ELEGANT SPLIT PEA SOUP
emerald green peas and white shell pasta make this special

1 (14 oz.) package green split peas, *soaked overnight in 5 cups water*
1-1/2 quarts (6 cups) basic vegetable *or* basic chicken stock (see pages 8, 9)
1 cup chopped celery and celery leaves
1-1/2 cups chopped carrots
1 cup chopped onions
1 cup chopped potatoes
3 large cloves garlic, minced

2 bay leaves
2 teaspoons salt
1/8 teaspoon pepper
1/2 teaspoon thyme
1-1/2 teaspoons dry mustard
1-1/2 cups cooked small shell pasta
1 cup fresh green peas, shelled, *or* 1 (10 oz.) package frozen peas

In a large kettle, combine the split peas, their soaking liquid, vegetable or chicken stock, celery, carrots, onions, potatoes, garlic, bay leaves, salt, pepper, thyme and dry mustard. Bring to a boil, reduce heat and simmer, covered, for 1-1/2 hours. Remove soup from heat and discard bay leaves. Purée the soup, a little at a time, in a food processor or an electric blender or by forcing through a strainer. Place puréed soup back into large kettle. Add shell pasta and green peas. Cook over medium heat until soup comes to a simmer, stirring occasionally. Makes 3-1/2 quarts.

GARBANZO BEAN SOUP
a meatless soup that is easy on your food budget

1-1/2 cups dried garbanzo beans, *soaked
   overnight in 3 cups water*
2 tablespoons butter or margarine
4 cloves garlic, minced
2 cups chopped onions
1/4 cup all-purpose flour
2 quarts (8 cups) water

1 cup chopped celery
1 cup chopped carrots
1 cup chopped fresh parsley
1 (16 oz.) can tomatoes, chopped, and their
   liquid
2 teaspoons salt
1/4 teaspoon pepper
1 teaspoon sage

In a bowl, combine garbanzo beans and 3 cups water; soak overnight. Next day, in a large kettle, melt butter or margarine and sauté garlic and onions until limp. Stir in flour and gradually mix in 2 quarts water. Add beans, their soaking liquid, celery, carrots, parsley, tomatoes and their liquid, salt, pepper and sage. Bring to a boil, reduce heat and simmer, covered, for 2 to 2-1/2 hours or until beans are very tender. Remove 4 cups of beans from soup, mash and return to kettle. Makes 4 quarts.

TANGY BEAN SOUP
wine vinegar gives this soup its zippy flavor

1 pound dried, small white beans, *soaked*
   overnight in 6 cups water
1-1/2 cups chopped onions
1 cup sliced celery
3 cloves garlic, minced
1/4 cup chopped fresh parsley
1 quart (4 cups) basic beef *or*
   basic vegetable stock (see pages 7, 9)

1 (16 oz.) can tomato purée
1 teaspoon salt
1/8 teaspoon pepper
1/2 teaspoon thyme
1/2 teaspoon basil
1/2 teaspoon oregano
1-1/2 cups diced potatoes
3 tablespoons wine vinegar

In a large kettle, combine the beans, their soaking liquid, onions, celery, garlic, parsley, beef or vegetable stock, tomato purée, salt, pepper, thyme, basil, and oregano; bring to boil. Reduce heat and simmer, covered, for 1-1/2 hours or until beans are almost completely tender. Add potatoes and continue to simmer an additional 20 minutes or until potatoes are tender. Add wine vinegar and simmer another 5 minutes. Makes 3 quarts.

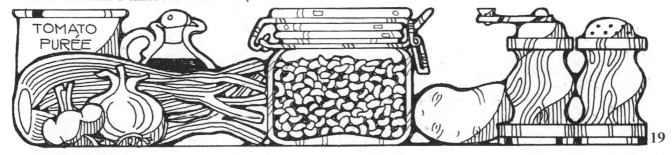

RICH, CREAMY SOUPS FOR A FROSTY EVENING

CONTINENTAL CHICKEN SOUP
an elegant version of creamed chicken soup

3 tablespoons butter or margarine
1-1/2 cups chopped onions
2 cups sliced celery
3/4 pound fresh mushrooms, sliced
3 tablespoons all-purpose flour
2 quarts (8 cups) basic chicken stock
  (see page 8)
2 teaspoons salt
1/8 teaspoon pepper

1/4 teaspoon nutmeg
1/2 teaspoon tarragon
3 cups diced cooked chicken
1 cup diced ham
2 egg yolks
1 cup half and half (light cream)
3 eggs, hard-cooked and grated
3 tablespoons lemon juice

In a large kettle, melt butter or margarine. Sauté onions, celery and mushrooms until onions are transparent. Stir in flour, add chicken stock, salt, pepper, nutmeg and tarragon. Bring to a boil, reduce heat and simmer, covered, for 20 minutes. Add chicken and ham. Simmer another 10 minutes. In a small bowl, combine egg yolks and half and half. Stir 1 cup of hot soup broth into this mixture. Stir cream mixture into soup. Reheat soup to serving temperature *but do not boil.* Just before serving, mix in grated eggs and lemon juice. Makes 4 quarts.

GREAT GREEN SOUP
a delicious gathering of green vegetables

3 tablespoons butter or margarine
1-1/2 cups chopped onions
1-1/2 cups sliced celery
1/2 cup chopped fresh parsley
3 quarts (12 cups) basic chicken stock
   (see page 8)
1-1/2 teaspoons salt
1/4 teaspoon pepper
1/2 teaspoon dill weed
1-1/2 cups (firmly packed) chopped spinach *or*
   1 (10 oz.) package frozen chopped spinach

1 cup (firmly packed) chopped escarole *or*
   1 (10 oz.) package frozen chopped escarole
1 pound fresh asparagus, trimmed and cut into
   1-inch pieces, *or* 1 (10 oz.) package frozen
   asparagus, cut into 1-inch pieces
1 cup cubed potatoes
1/4 cup white rice
2 egg yolks
1 cup half and half (light cream)

In a large kettle, melt butter or margarine and sauté the onions, celery and parsley until onions are transparent. Add chicken stock, salt, pepper, dill weed, spinach, escarole, asparagus pieces, potatoes and rice. Bring to a boil, reduce heat and simmer, covered, for 30 minutes. In a small bowl, combine egg yolks and half and half. Stir 1 cup of hot soup broth into this mixture. Stir cream mixture into soup. Reheat soup to serving temperature *but do not boil.* Makes 4 quarts.

SPINACH SOUP
garnish each bowl with slices of hard-cooked eggs

1/3 cup butter or margarine
1 cup chopped onions
2 cloves garlic, minced
2 quarts (8 cups) basic chicken stock
   (see page 8)
2 pounds fresh spinach, chopped *or*
   2 (10 oz.) packages frozen, chopped
   spinach

1-1/2 teaspoons salt
1/4 teaspoon paprika
1/4 teaspoon mace
1/4 teaspoon thyme
1/3 cup all-purpose flour
3 cups half and half (light cream)
2 egg yolks
hard-cooked eggs, for garnish

In a large kettle, melt the butter or margarine. Sauté onions and garlic until limp. Add chicken stock, spinach, salt, paprika, mace and thyme. Bring to a boil, reduce heat and simmer, covered, for 25 minutes. In a small bowl, mix flour with half and half until well blended; add egg yolks and stir well. Stir egg mixture into soup and continue to heat, stirring occasionally, to serving temperature. *Do not boil.* Before serving, garnish with slices of hard-cooked eggs. Makes 3 quarts.

GOULASH SOUP
a favorite dish of Hungarian peasants and herdsmen

2 pounds lean beef, cut into 1-inch cubes
2 tablespoons butter or margarine
3 cups sliced onions
4 cloves garlic, minced
2 tablespoons paprika
2 quarts (8 cups) basic beef stock (see page 7)
1 (16 oz.) can tomatoes, chopped, and their
   liquid

1 cup chopped fresh tomatoes
1/2 cup dry white wine
1 tablespoon salt
1/4 teaspoon pepper
3 cups diced potatoes
1/2 pound fresh mushrooms, thinly sliced
1 cup sour cream
2 tablespoons all-purpose flour

In a large kettle, brown the beef in the butter or margarine. Add onions and garlic; sauté until the onions are limp. Sprinkle the paprika over all and mix well. Add the beef stock, canned tomatoes, fresh tomatoes, wine, salt and pepper; bring to a boil. Reduce heat and simmer, covered, for 2 hours or until beef is tender. Add potatoes and mushrooms; simmer 15 minutes longer or until potatoes are tender. In a small bowl, combine sour cream and flour thoroughly; mix 1/2 cup of the soup broth into sour cream mixture. Stir sour cream mixture into soup; reheat soup to serving temperature *but do not boil.* Makes 4 quarts.

BARLEY, VEAL AND VEGETABLE SOUP
a hearty peasant soup with origins in Poland

2 tablespoons butter or margarine
2-1/2 pounds boneless veal, cut into 3/4-inch
  cubes
2-1/2 quarts (10 cups) basic chicken stock
  (see page 8)
1/2 cup pearl barley
1-1/2 cups chopped onions
2 teaspoons salt
1/2 teaspoon thyme

3 whole cloves
1 bay leaf
1-1/2 cups thinly sliced carrots
1 cup thinly sliced celery
1/2 pound fresh mushrooms, thinly sliced
1 tablespoon lemon juice
2 egg yolks
1 cup half and half (light cream)

In a large kettle, melt butter or margarine and brown the veal. Add chicken stock, barley, onions, salt, thyme, whole cloves and bay leaf. Bring to a boil, reduce heat and simmer, covered, for 1-1/2 hours or until meat is tender. Add carrots and celery. Continue to simmer for 15 minutes. Add mushrooms and simmer for an additional 10 minutes. In a small bowl, combine lemon juice, egg yolks and half and half. Stir 1 cup of hot soup broth into this mixture. Add cream mixture to soup in kettle, stirring until smooth. Heat to serving temperature *but do not boil.* Makes 4 quarts.

MULLIGATAWNY
a curried soup from southern India

1 chicken (about 2-1/2 to 3 lbs.), cut up
1/3 cup all-purpose flour
1 teaspoon paprika
1/3 cup butter or margarine
1-1/2 cups chopped onions
1-1/2 cups chopped celery
1 cup chopped carrots
1 cup chopped, unpeeled, tart apples
1 tablespoon salt

2 tablespoons curry powder
1 teaspoon mace
1/2 teaspoon thyme leaves
2 quarts (8 cups) basic chicken stock
  (see page 8)
1/2 cup flaked coconut
1 cup unsweetened apple juice
1 cup half and half (light cream)
3 cups cooked, hot rice

Coat chicken pieces with a mixture of flour and paprika. Reserve remaining coating mixture for later use. In a large kettle, melt butter or margarine. Thoroughly brown chicken pieces on all sides. Remove from kettle and set aside. In kettle sauté onions, celery, carrots and apples until onions are limp. Sprinkle salt, curry powder, mace, thyme and reserved flour mixture over sautéed vegetables. Stir to combine thoroughly. Gradually add chicken stock, stirring until smooth. Add chicken pieces and coconut. Bring to a boil, reduce heat and simmer, covered, for 1 hour or until chicken is tender, stirring occasionally. Remove chicken and set aside to cool. Skim any excess fat from top of soup. Place soup (two or three cups at a time) in a food processor or electric blender and blend until smooth. Return soup to kettle. When chicken pieces are cool enough to handle, discard skin and bones. Cut meat into bite-size pieces and add to soup along with apple juice and half and half. Mix thoroughly. Add rice. Reheat to serving temperature, *but do not boil.* Makes 4 quarts.

SALAMI CHOWDER
the whole family will love this great soup

3 tablespoons butter or margarine
1/2 pound dry salami, chopped
1-1/2 cups chopped onions
3 cloves garlic, minced
1 cup chopped celery
1 cup coarsely shredded carrots
2 cups coarsely shredded cabbage
2 quarts (8 cups) basic beef stock (see page 7)

1-1/2 teaspoons salt
1/8 teaspoon pepper
1 teaspoon savory
1/2 teaspoon oregano
1/2 cup macaroni
1 cup chopped spinach, fresh or frozen
1 pint (2 cups) half and half (light cream)
1/2 cup Parmesan or Romano cheese

In a large kettle, melt the butter or margarine; sauté salami until it begins to get crisp, about 2 minutes. Add onions, garlic, celery, carrots and cabbage; sauté 1 minute. Add beef stock, salt, pepper, savory and oregano; bring the soup to boil. Reduce heat and simmer, covered, for 30 minutes. Add macaroni and spinach; simmer for 15 minutes longer or until macaroni is tender. Stir in the half and half and cheese; reheat to serving temperature *but do not boil*. Makes 3-1/2 quarts.

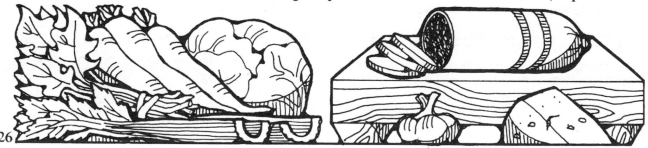

CORN AND FRANK CHOWDER
this chunky soup could brighten a rainy day

1-1/2 cups chopped onions
2 cups sliced celery
2 cups chopped potatoes
3 cups water
2 teaspoons salt
1/2 teaspoon paprika
1/4 teaspoon thyme
1/2 teaspoon dry mustard
1 small bay leaf

2 (17 oz.) cans cut corn, drained
  or 3 cups cut, fresh corn
3 cups cold milk
1/4 cup all-purpose flour
1 (17 oz.) can cream style corn
1 teaspoon Worcestershire sauce
1/2 pound frankfurters, sliced
3 cups shredded medium or sharp
  cheddar cheese

In a large kettle, combine onions, celery, potatoes, water, salt, paprika, thyme, dry mustard and bay leaf. Bring to a boil, reduce heat and simmer, uncovered, for about 15 minutes. Add cut corn and simmer, uncovered, for another 15 minutes. In a small bowl, mix together the cold milk and flour until smooth. To soup, add cream style corn, milk mixture, Worcestershire sauce and frankfurters. Stir in cheese until smooth. Bring soup to serving temperature *but do not boil.* Makes 4 quarts.

CHICKEN CHOWDER
garnish this soup with crumbled bacon

2 tablespoons butter or margarine
1-1/2 cups chopped onions
2 cups sliced celery
1-1/2 quarts (6 cups) basic chicken stock
  (see page 8)
1 (16 oz.) can stewed tomatoes and their
  liquid
2 teaspoons salt
1/4 teaspoon pepper

1 tablespoon Worcestershire sauce
2 cups fresh lima beans *or*
  1 (10 oz.) package frozen baby lima beans
1/2 cup white rice
1-1/2 cups cubed potatoes
1 (17 oz.) can cream style corn
1 pint (2 cups) half and half (light cream)
2-1/2 cups diced, cooked chicken
crumbled bacon, for garnish

In a large kettle, melt the butter or margarine; sauté onions and celery until onions are limp. Add the chicken stock, stewed tomatoes, their liquid, salt, pepper, Worcestershire sauce, lima beans, rice and potatoes; bring to a boil. Reduce heat and simmer, covered, for 30 minutes or until beans, rice and potatoes are tender. Add corn, half and half, and chicken. Reheat soup to serving temperature but *do not boil.* Before serving, garnish soup with crumbled bacon. Makes 4 quarts.

CURRIED POTATO AND MUSHROOM CHOWDER
curry adds a touch of India to this velvety soup

1 pound fresh mushrooms, sliced
3 to 5 leeks, well rinsed and sliced thin
    (about 2 cups)
2 cups sliced celery
1/2 cup butter or margarine
4 cups cubed potatoes
1 quart (4 cups) water

2-1/2 teaspoons salt
2 cups milk
2 egg yolks, beaten
1 pint (2 cups) sour cream
1/4 cup all-purpose flour
1/4 cup dry white wine
2 teaspoons curry powder

In a large kettle, sauté the mushrooms, leeks and celery in butter or margarine for 3 to 4 minutes. Add potatoes, water and salt. Bring to a boil, reduce heat and simmer, uncovered, for 15 minutes or until potatoes are tender. Add milk and stir. In a small bowl, combine egg yolks and sour cream. Add flour and stir until smooth. Add wine and stir until smooth. Stir sour cream mixture into soup and add curry powder. Reheat soup to serving temperature *but do not boil.* Makes 3-1/2 quarts.

29

BAKED BEAN CHOWDER
an easy-to-make soup that features canned baked beans

1/4 pound bacon, diced
2 cups chopped onions
1 cup thinly sliced celery
1 quart (4 cups) basic beef stock (see page 7)
2 (29 oz.) cans baked beans
3 cups diced potatoes
1-1/2 teaspoons salt
1/4 teaspoon pepper
1 teaspoon thyme
1/2 teaspoon savory
1 cup half and half (light cream)

In a large kettle, cook bacon over medium heat until it is crisp. Remove and drain on paper towels; set aside. Sauté onions and celery in bacon drippings in kettle. Add beef stock, baked beans, potatoes, salt, pepper, thyme, and savory. Bring to a boil, reduce heat and simmer, covered, for 30 minutes or until potatoes are tender. Add half and half and reheat to serving temperature, *but do not boil.* Sprinkle reserved bacon pieces on top of each serving. Makes 4 quarts.

SUPER SOUPS MADE WITH MEATS & POULTRY

HAMBURGER SOUP
a quick and easy soup to make on busy days

1 pound lean ground beef
2-1/2 quarts (10 cups) basic beef stock (see page 7)
1 (28 oz.) can tomatoes, chopped, and their liquid
1 cup chopped onions
1 cup sliced carrots
1/2 cup sliced celery

1/2 cup pearl barley
1 tablespoon garlic salt
1 tablespoon basil
1 teaspoon ground oregano
1/2 pound zucchini, sliced
1/4 pound vermicelli, broken
1/4 cup grated Romano or Parmesan cheese

In a large skillet, brown ground beef and drain thoroughly. In a large kettle, combine the drained beef, beef stock, tomatoes, their liquid, onions, carrots, celery, barley, garlic salt, basil and oregano. Bring to a boil, reduce heat, cover and simmer for 45 minutes or until barley is tender. Add zucchini and vermicelli and continue to simmer for 10 minutes or until vermicelli is tender. Add cheese and serve. Makes 4 quarts.

TACO SOUP
a tasty adaptation of the ever-popular Mexican taco

1 pound lean ground beef
2-1/2 quarts (10 cups) basic chicken stock
   (see page 8)
1 (2-1/2 oz.) package taco seasoning mix
1/2 teaspoon cumin
1/2 teaspoon salt
1/4 teaspoon pepper
1 cup thinly sliced green onion
2 cups chopped fresh tomatoes
1 (15 oz.) can pitted black olives, drained
   and sliced
shredded iceberg lettuce and corn chips,
   for garnish

In a medium size skillet, brown the ground beef. Drain well and set aside. In a large kettle, combine the chicken stock, taco seasoning mix, cumin, salt, pepper and browned ground beef. Bring to a boil. Reduce heat and simmer, covered, for 10 minutes. Add green onion, tomatoes and black olives. Simmer another 10 minutes. When serving, add shredded lettuce and corn chips to each bowl. Makes 3-1/2 quarts.

HOLIDAY MEATBALL SOUP
adapted from a recipe for an Italian wedding soup

3/4 pound lean ground beef
1/4 cup finely minced onion
1/4 cup finely minced fresh parsley
1/4 cup fine, dry bread crumbs
1 teaspoon garlic salt
3 tablespoons grated Romano *or*
　Parmesan cheese
1 egg

3 tablespoons milk
2-1/2 quarts (10 cups) basic chicken stock
　(see page 8)
1 (8 oz.) can tomato sauce
1/2 teaspoon salt
1/8 teaspoon pepper
3 cups (packed) chopped endive *or* escarole
2 eggs, beaten

In a medium size bowl, combine ground beef, onion, parsley, bread crumbs, garlic salt, cheese, 1 egg and milk. Work with hands to mix thoroughly. Form meat mixture into 60 one-inch meatballs. Brown the meatballs in a large skillet and drain on paper towels. Set aside. In a large kettle, combine chicken stock, tomato sauce, salt and pepper. Bring to a boil, reduce heat, add meatballs and simmer, covered, for 30 minutes. While soup is simmering, in a saucepan heat 1/2 cup water to boiling and cook endive or escarole for 5 minutes or until tender. Drain endive or escarole thoroughly and add to soup. Allow soup to come to a simmer again. Now, with soup simmering, pour a little of the beaten egg mixture slowly in a fine stream into the soup. With a fork in the other hand, make wide circles on the surface of the soup to catch the egg and draw it into long, filmy threads. Continue this procedure until all egg is added and cooked. Simmer for an additional 1 minute. Makes 3 quarts.

MEATBALL TAGLIARINI SOUP

sprinkle a dash of Parmesan cheese on each bowl

1 pound lean ground beef
2 ounces sliced ham, finely minced
3 cloves garlic, very finely minced
1/4 cup finely minced fresh parsley
1/3 cup finely minced green onion
1/2 cup grated Parmesan cheese
1/2 cup dry bread crumbs
1 teaspoon salt
1/4 teaspoon lemon pepper
3/4 cup milk

1 egg
1 tablespoon butter or margarine
2 quarts (8 cups) basic beef stock (see page 7)
1/4 cup chopped fresh parsley
7 cups water
3 tablespoons instant beef bouillon (or beef
  bouillon cubes)
1 (12 oz.) package egg tagliarini, broken
  in small pieces
Parmesan cheese, for garnish

In a bowl, thoroughly combine beef, ham, garlic, 1/4 cup parsley, onion, Parmesan cheese, bread crumbs, salt, lemon pepper, milk and egg; form into about 50 meatballs. In a large kettle, brown the meatballs in the butter or margarine; remove and drain on paper towels. Pour all fat out of the kettle; add beef stock, 1/4 cup parsley, water and beef bouillon. Bring mixture to a boil; add meatballs, reduce heat and simmer, covered, for 20 minutes. Add the broken tagliarini and continue to simmer for 10 minutes more or until pasta is tender. Serve with a dash of Parmesan cheese in each serving. Makes 4 quarts.

EGGPLANT AND MEATBALL SOUP
a pleasing combination of vegetables, meat and pasta

3/4 pound lean ground beef
1/4 cup dry bread crumbs
1/4 cup milk
2 teaspoons Worcestershire sauce
1/4 cup minced onion
2 teaspoons parsley flakes
1/2 teaspoon salt
1/2 teaspoon chili powder
1/4 teaspoon garlic powder
2 quarts (8 cups) basic beef stock (see page 7)
1 (28 oz.) can tomatoes, chopped, and their
  liquid

1 cup chopped onions
3 cloves garlic, minced
1 cup sliced celery
1/2 cup chopped green pepper
1 teaspoon salt
1/4 teaspoon nutmeg
1/4 teaspoon marjoram
1 (1-1/2 lb.) unpeeled eggplant,
  cut into 1-inch cubes
1/2 cup small elbow macaroni

In a medium size bowl, combine the ground beef, bread crumbs, milk, Worcestershire sauce, minced onion, parsley flakes, salt, chili powder and garlic powder. Work with hands to mix thoroughly. Form meat mixture into about 25 meatballs. Brown the meatballs in a large skillet and drain on paper towels. Set aside. In a large kettle, combine the beef stock, tomatoes, their liquid, onions, garlic, celery, green pepper, salt, nutmeg and marjoram. Bring to a boil, add the meatballs, reduce heat and simmer, covered, for 15 minutes. Add the eggplant and simmer, covered, for another 15 minutes. Add macaroni and simmer, covered, for 15 minutes or until macaroni is tender. Makes 3-1/2 quarts.

CHILE BEEF SOUP
a spicy-hot soup for that casual big dinner

3/4 pound dried red beans, *soaked overnight
  in 4 cups water*
2 tablespoons butter or margarine
1-1/2 pounds lean beef, cut into 1/2-inch cubes
1-1/2 quarts (6 cups) basic beef stock
  (see page 7)
3 cloves garlic, minced
1 cup chopped onions
1 (4 oz.) can chopped green chiles
1 (28 oz.) can tomatoes, chopped, with their
  liquid
1-1/2 teaspoons salt
1 teaspoon cumin
1 cup small elbow macaroni

Place beans in bowl, add water and soak overnight. Next day, in a large kettle, melt butter or margarine. Brown the beef and add red beans, their soaking liquid, beef stock, garlic, onions, chiles, tomatoes, their liquid, salt and cumin. Bring to a boil, reduce heat and simmer, covered, for 2 hours or until beans and meat are tender. Add macaroni and continue to simmer for 10 minutes or until macaroni is tender. Makes 4 quarts.

ALPHABET SOUP WITH BEEF
a super thick soup that satisfies the heartiest of appetites

1-1/2 pounds beef neck bones
2 quarts (8 cups) water
1 tablespoon salt
3/4 cup chopped onions
1/4 cup green split peas
1/4 cup pearl barley
1/4 cup brown rice

1 cup chopped celery
1 cup chopped carrots
1/2 cup chopped fresh parsley
1 (16 oz.) can tomatoes and their liquid
1/2 cup alphabet macaroni
1/4 teaspoon pepper

In a large kettle, combine neck bones, water, salt and onions and bring to a boil. Add split peas, barley and brown rice. Stir well, cover and simmer for 1 hour. Add celery, carrots and parsley. Simmer, covered, for an additional hour. Remove neck bones from soup; cut meat into bite size pieces and return to soup. Cut canned tomatoes into small pieces and add to soup along with the tomato liquid. Bring soup to a boil, add alphabet macaroni and pepper. Simmer, covered, for 15 minutes, stirring occasionally. Makes 3 quarts.

BEEF AND OKRA SOUP
float croutons on top of this colorful soup

1 pound lean beef, cut into 1-inch cubes
2 tablespoons butter or margarine
1 quart (4 cups) basic beef stock (see page 7)
1 cup water
1 (16 oz.) can tomatoes, chopped, and their
  liquid
1 cup chopped onions
1/4 teaspoon marjoram
1 bay leaf
1 teaspoon salt

1/4 teaspoon pepper
2 cups fresh lima beans *or*
  1 (10 oz.) package frozen lima beans
1 pound fresh spinach, chopped *or*
  1 (10 oz.) package frozen, chopped spinach
1 pound fresh, small okra *or* 1 (1 lb.) package
  frozen okra, sliced crosswise into 1/2-inch rings
1/2 cup thinly sliced green onion
1/2 pound ham, diced
croutons, for garnish

In a large kettle, brown beef in butter or margarine. Add beef stock, water, tomatoes and their liquid, onions, marjoram, bay leaf, salt and pepper. Bring to a boil, reduce heat and simmer, covered, for 1-1/2 hours or until beef is tender. Add lima beans and spinach. Simmer another 30 minutes or until lima beans are tender. Add okra and green onion and simmer an additional 30 minutes or until okra is tender. Finally, add ham and stir. Garnish with croutons. Makes 3 quarts.

HOMINY SOUP WITH BEEF AND PORK
a popular dish in the Southwest U.S.A.

2 tablespoons butter or margarine
1/2 pound lean beef, cut into 1/2-inch cubes
1/2 pound lean pork, cut into 1/2-inch cubes
1-1/2 quarts (6 cups) basic beef stock (see
   page 7)
1 (28 oz.) can tomatoes, chopped, and their
   liquid
1-1/2 cups chopped onions
2 teaspoons salt
1/4 teaspoon crushed, dried red peppers
1/4 teaspoon cumin
1-1/2 cups cubed potatoes
3/4 pound yellow crookneck squash, cut into
   1-inch cubes *or* 1 (10 oz.) package frozen
   crookneck squash
1 (29 oz.) can golden yellow hominy, undrained

In a large kettle, melt butter or margarine and brown the beef and pork. Add beef stock, tomatoes, their liquid, onions, salt, crushed red pepper and cumin. Bring to a boil, reduce heat and simmer, covered, for 2 hours or until meats are tender. Add potatoes, squash and hominy. Continue to simmer for 20 minutes or just until vegetables are tender. Makes 4 quarts.

MEATY VEGETABLE SOUP WITH SAUERKRAUT
generous servings of this taste great on a cold winter day

2 tablespoons butter or margarine
1 pound lean beef, cut into 1-inch cubes
1/2 pound lean pork, cut into 1-inch cubes
2 quarts (8 cups) basic beef stock
   (see page 7)
1 (16 oz.) can tomatoes, chopped, and their
   liquid
1 (16 oz.) can sauerkraut, undrained
1-1/2 cups chopped onions
1-1/2 cups chopped celery

1 cup sliced carrots
1/2 cup chopped fresh parsley
3 cloves garlic, minced
1 bay leaf
2 teaspoons salt
1/4 teaspoon pepper
1/2 teaspoon marjoram
1/4 teaspoon thyme
2 tablespoons packed brown sugar

In a large kettle, melt butter or margarine; brown the beef and pork. Add beef stock, tomatoes and their liquid, undrained sauerkraut, onions, celery, carrots, parsley, garlic, bay leaf, salt, pepper, marjoram, and thyme. Bring to a boil, reduce heat and simmer, covered, for 2 hours or until meat is tender. Stir in brown sugar and simmer, covered, an additional 15 minutes. Makes 4 quarts.

FRANKFURTER RICE SOUP
make this ahead and take it along on camping trips

2 tablespoons butter or margarine
1 cup chopped onions
1 cup chopped green pepper
1-1/2 cups sliced celery
1/2 cup chopped fresh parsley
2 quarts (8 cups) basic chicken stock
   (see page 8)
1 (28 oz.) can stewed tomatoes

2 teaspoons salt
1/4 teaspoon pepper
1/2 teaspoon dill weed
1 bay leaf
1/2 cup brown rice
1/2 pound frankfurters, sliced
1 (10 oz.) package frozen green peas

In a large kettle, melt butter or margarine; sauté onions, green pepper, celery and parsley until onions are transparent. Add chicken stock, stewed tomatoes, salt, pepper, dill weed, bay leaf and brown rice; bring to a boil. Reduce heat and simmer, covered, for 45 minutes. Add sliced frankfurters and peas; continue to simmer another 10 minutes. Makes 4 quarts.

41

BEEF SHANK MINESTRONE
in northern Italy rice is used instead of pasta

1/2 pound dried pink beans, *soaked overnight in 3 cups water*
2 pounds beef shanks
2 tablespoons cooking oil
2 quarts (8 cups) basic beef stock (see page 7)
1 cup chopped red Italian onions
1/2 cup chopped fresh parsley
3 cloves garlic, minced
1 teaspoon basil
1/2 teaspoon thyme
2 teaspoons salt

1/4 teaspoon pepper
1 (16 oz.) can tomatoes, chopped, and their liquid
1 cup chopped carrots
1 cup sliced celery
1/2 cup brown rice
1 cup diced potatoes
1 cup fresh, cut green beans
   or 1/2 (10 oz.) package frozen cut green beans
1/2 pound cabbage, shredded

Place pink beans in a bowl, add 3 cups water and soak overnight. Next day, in a large kettle, brown beef shanks in oil; add pink beans, their soaking liquid, beef stock, onions, parsley, garlic, basil, thyme, salt and pepper. Bring to a boil. Reduce heat and simmer, covered, for 2 hours or until beans are slightly tender. Remove beef shanks, and cut any meat off, returning meat to soup. Add tomatoes, their liquid, carrots, celery and rice. Simmer another 45 minutes. Add potatoes, green beans and cabbage. Simmer an additional 15 minutes or until potatoes are tender. Makes 4 quarts.

VEAL PASTA MINESTRONE
a favorite Italian soup the world over

1 pound dried kidney beans, *soaked
  overnight in 6 cups water*
2 pounds veal shanks
2 tablespoons butter or margarine
2 quarts (8 cups) basic chicken stock
  or water
1-1/2 cups chopped red Italian onions
3 cloves garlic, minced
1 teaspoon basil
1 teaspoon oregano

2 teaspoons salt
1/4 teaspoon pepper
2 bay leaves
2 cups (packed) chopped chicory *or*
  romaine lettuce
1 cup chopped celery
3/4 cup small elbow or salad macaroni
1/2 pound mushrooms, sliced
1/2 pound zucchini, sliced
1/2 cup dry sherry (optional)

The night before, soak beans in 6 cups water. The next day, in a large kettle brown the veal shanks in butter or margarine. Add the chicken stock, onions, garlic, basil, oregano, salt, pepper and bay leaves. Bring to a boil. Reduce heat and simmer, covered, for 1 1/2 hours or until meat is tender. Remove veal shanks and cut meat off, returning meat to soup. Add chicory or romaine, celery and kidney beans and their soaking liquid. Continue to simmer another 1 hour or until beans are tender. Add small elbow or salad macaroni, mushrooms and zucchini. Simmer an additional 10 minutes or until macaroni is tender. If desired, add sherry just before serving. Makes 4 quarts.

PEASANT BORSCHT
garnish each bowl with sour cream and chopped, fresh parsley

1/2 pound dried small white beans, *soaked overnight in 3 cups water*
3/4 pound beef neck bones
3/4 pound country style pork spareribs, trimmed of excess fat
2 quarts (8 cups) water
4 tablespoons instant beef bouillon (or 4 beef bouillon cubes)
1 cup chopped onions
4 cloves garlic, minced
2 bay leaves

1 cup diced carrots
1 (16 oz.) can tomato purée
1 (16 oz.) can shoestring beets and their liquid
2 cups (1/2 lb.) chopped cabbage
1/4 cup vinegar
2 tablespoons brown sugar
1 teaspoon salt
1/4 teaspoon pepper
sour cream and chopped, fresh parsley, for garnish

In a large kettle, combine beans, their soaking liquid, beef neck bones, pork spareribs, water, bouillon, onions, garlic, bay leaves and carrots. Heat to boiling, cover, reduce heat and simmer for 1-1/2 hours. Remove meat and bones from soup. Cut meat into bite size pieces and return to soup. Add tomato purée, beets and their liquid, cabbage, vinegar, brown sugar, salt and pepper. Continue to simmer, covered, for another 30 minutes. Garnish each serving with sour cream and chopped, fresh parsley. Makes 4 quarts.

CANADIAN PEA SOUP
traditionally made with yellow split peas and served unstrained

1 pound yellow split peas, *soaked overnight in 6 cups water*
1 (1-1/2 lb.) meaty ham bone
1-1/2 quarts (6 cups) water
2 cups chopped onions
3 cloves garlic, minced
1 large bay leaf
1 cup sliced celery
1 cup diced carrots
1 cup diced turnips
2 teaspoons savory
1 tablespoon salt
1/2 teaspoon pepper
1 (12 oz.) can beer

In a large kettle, combine split peas, their soaking liquid, ham bone, water, onions, garlic, bay leaf, celery, carrots, and turnips; bring to a boil. Reduce heat, cover and simmer for 2 to 2-1/2 hours or until peas have completely disintegrated. Remove ham bone from soup; cut meat in bite-size pieces and return meat to kettle along with savory, salt, pepper and beer. Simmer, covered, for 30 minutes longer, stirring occasionally. Makes 3-1/2 quarts.

GREAT NORTHERN BEAN SOUP
serve steaming bowls of this after the football game

3/4 pound dried Great Northern beans, *soaked
  overnight in 4 cups water*
1 (1-1/2 lb.) meaty ham bone
2 quarts (8 cups) basic chicken stock
  (see page 8)
1-1/2 cups chopped red Italian onions
1-1/2 cups sliced celery
1-1/2 cups sliced carrots

4 cloves garlic, minced
1-1/2 teaspoons salt
1/4 teaspoon pepper
1/4 teaspoon marjoram
1/4 teaspoon thyme
2 bay leaves
1 cup diced turnips
1/2 pound cabbage, chopped

In a large kettle, combine the Great Northern beans, their soaking liquid, the ham bone, chicken stock, onions, celery, carrots, garlic, salt, pepper, marjoram, thyme and bay leaves. Bring to a boil, reduce heat and simmer, covered, for 1 hour or until beans are tender. Remove ham bone and cut any meat off, returning meat to soup. Add turnips and cabbage to soup. Continue to simmer, covered, for another 30 minutes or until turnips are tender. Makes 4 quarts.

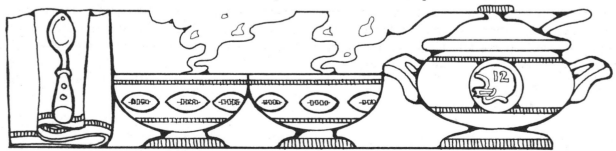

ZUCCHINI AND BACON SOUP
this soup is even better the second day

1 pound bacon, chopped
1-1/2 cups chopped onions
1 cup sliced celery
1/2 cup chopped fresh parsley
4 cloves garlic, minced
3 pounds zucchini, sliced
2 quarts (8 cups) basic beef stock (see page 7)
2 teaspoons salt
1/4 teaspoon pepper
1 teaspoon basil
1/2 teaspoon thyme

In a large kettle, fry the bacon until it is crisp; drain on paper towels. Discard all but about 3 tablespoons of the bacon fat. Sauté onions, celery, parsley and garlic in reserved bacon fat. Add zucchini, beef stock, salt, pepper, basil and thyme; bring to a boil. Reduce heat and simmer, covered, for 30 minutes. Purée the soup, a little at a time, in a food processor, an electric blender or by forcing through a strainer. Place puréed soup back into kettle. Add crisp bacon and reheat soup. Makes 3-1/2 quarts.

LIMA BEAN AND SAUSAGE SOUP
carrots and tomatoes add colorful accents

1/2 pound dried lima beans, *soaked overnight in 3 cups water*
1 quart (4 cups) water
1 (16 oz.) can stewed tomatoes and their liquid
1 cup chopped onions
1 cup chopped celery
1 cup chopped carrots
1/2 cup chopped fresh parsley
1 cup chopped romaine lettuce or escarole

1-1/2 teaspoons salt
1/4 teaspoon pepper
1/4 teaspoon marjoram
1/4 teaspoon thyme
1/4 teaspoon oregano
1/2 pound bulk sausage meat
1/3 cup cracker crumbs
1 tablespoon milk
1 egg

In a large kettle, combine lima beans, their soaking liquid, water, stewed tomatoes, their liquid, onions, celery, carrots, parsley, romaine lettuce, salt, pepper, marjoram, thyme and oregano. Bring to a boil, reduce heat and simmer, covered, for 1 hour or until beans are tender. While soup is simmering, combine sausage meat, cracker crumbs, milk and egg in a mixing bowl. Form mixture into 25 one-inch meatballs. In a medium size skillet, brown meatballs and drain on paper towel. Add meatballs to soup and continue to simmer for 20 minutes. Makes 3 quarts.

MULTIPLE BEAN WITH SAUSAGE SOUP

sausage gives a spicy tang to this soup

3/4 cup dried pinto beans
3/4 cup dried pink beans
1/2 cup dried green split peas
1/2 cup dried lentils
1/2 cup pearl barley
4-1/2 quarts (18 cups) water
1 (16 oz.) can tomato purée
2 cups chopped onions
1 pound Italian sausage links, mild or hot
2 bay leaves
2 teaspoons basil leaves
1 tablespoon salt
1/2 teaspoon pepper
2 cups chopped potatoes

The night before, combine pinto beans, pink beans, split peas, lentils, barley and 3 quarts (12 cups) water in a large kettle; soak overnight. The next day, add remaining 1-1/2 quarts (6 cups) water, tomato purée and onions. Bring to a boil. Add sausage, bay leaves, basil, salt and pepper. Reduce heat, cover and simmer for 1 to 2 hours, or until beans are tender. Remove sausage from soup and cut into thin slices. Return meat to soup. Add potatoes, cover and simmer for 20 minutes, stirring occasionally. Makes 4 quarts.

LIMA BEAN LAMB SOUP
this delicious combination is high in protein

1 pound dried lima beans, *soaked overnight in 6 cups water*
1 meaty leftover leg of lamb bone *or* 1-1/2 pounds lamb neck bones
1-1/2 quarts (6 cups) water
1-1/2 cups chopped onions
2 cups chopped celery
3 cloves garlic, minced
2 teaspoons salt
1/4 teaspoon pepper
1 teaspoon crushed rosemary
1 (15 oz.) can tomato sauce
2 cups chopped escarole

In a large kettle, combine the lima beans, their soaking liquid, the leg of lamb bone or lamb neck bones, water, onions, celery, garlic, salt, pepper and rosemary; bring to a boil. Reduce heat and simmer, covered, for 1 hour or until beans are very tender. Remove bone and cut any meat off, returning meat to soup. Add tomato sauce and escarole; continue to simmer, covered, for another 30 minutes. If an unusually large amount of fat seems to have accumulated on top of soup, skim it off and discard. Makes 4 quarts.

LAMB AND CABBAGE SOUP
a favorite soup in Scandanavian countries

1 meaty leftover leg of lamb bone *or* 1-1/2 pounds
   lamb neck bones
2 quarts (8 cups) basic beef stock (see page 7)
2 teaspoons salt
1/8 teaspoon pepper
1/2 teaspoon allspice
1-1/2 cups sliced leeks
1 cup diced turnips
1 cup sliced carrots
1 cup sliced celery
1/4 cup chopped fresh parsley
1 cup diced potatoes
1 (1-1/2 lb.) head cabbage, shredded

In a large kettle, combine the lamb bone, beef stock, salt, pepper and allspice. Bring soup to a boil. Reduce heat and simmer, covered, for 2 hours or until meat is tender. Remove lamb bone and cut any meat off, returning meat to soup. Add leeks, turnips, carrots, celery and parsley. Simmer 15 minutes. Add potatoes and cabbage and simmer an additional 20 minutes, or until potatoes are tender. Makes 3 quarts.

HEARTY CHICKEN SOUP
a delicious way to utilize leftover chicken

1 medium size (3/4 lb.) celery root, peeled
    and chopped
1 cup chopped onions
1 cup chopped carrots
1/4 cup chopped fresh parsley
2-1/2 quarts (10 cups) basic chicken stock
    (see page 8)
1 (16 oz.) can stewed tomatoes and their liquid

2 cloves garlic, minced
1 teaspoon salt
1/2 teaspoon ground thyme
1/4 teaspoon ground cardamom
1/8 teaspoon allspice
2 cups chopped, cooked chicken
4 ounces fine egg noodles

In a large kettle, combine celery root, onions, carrots, parsley, chicken stock, stewed tomatoes and their liquid, garlic, salt, thyme, cardamom and allspice. Bring to a boil, reduce heat, cover and simmer for 1 to 1-1/2 hours. Add chicken and noodles. Cook over medium-high heat until noodles are tender, stirring occasionally. Makes 4 quarts.

ORIENTAL CHICKEN VEGETABLE SOUP
very colorful and full of slightly crisp vegetables

2-1/2 quarts (10 cups) basic chicken stock (see page 8)
3 cloves garlic, finely minced
2 teaspoons salt
2 cups thinly sliced celery
2 cups thinly sliced carrots
1 cup peeled and thinly sliced broccoli stems
1/2 pound cabbage, finely shredded
2 cups cooked and diced chicken
1 (8 oz.) can water chestnuts, drained and thinly sliced
1 cup thinly sliced green onions
1-1/2 cups fresh green peas, shelled *or*
    1 (10 oz.) package frozen green peas

In a large kettle, combine the chicken stock, garlic and salt; bring to a boil. Add the celery, carrots, broccoli, cabbage and chicken. After this comes to a boil, reduce heat and simmer, covered, for 3 minutes. Add the water chestnuts, green onions and green peas; continue to simmer, covered, for another 3 to 5 minutes. Makes 4 quarts.

CHICKEN DUMPLING SOUP
the chicken is right in the dumpling

Chicken dumplings:
- 3 cups minced, cooked chicken
- 2 eggs
- 4-3/4 cups basic chicken stock
  (see page 8)
- 1 cup all-purpose flour
- 1/4 cup chopped fresh parsley
- 2 teaspoons salt
- 1/8 teaspoon pepper
- 1/2 teaspoon tarragon

Soup:
- 2 cups chopped onions
- 1-1/2 cups thinly sliced celery
- 2 cloves garlic, minced
- 1/4 cup butter or margarine
- 1/2 cup all-purpose flour
- 2 quarts (8 cups) basic chicken stock
  (see page 8)
- 1-1/2 teaspoons salt
- 1-1/2 cups shredded carrots
- 1-1/2 cups shredded cucumbers

To make chicken dumplings, combine the chicken, eggs, 3/4 cup chicken stock, flour, parsley, salt, pepper and tarragon in an electric blender or food processor; blend at high speed until smooth. In a medium size kettle, bring 4 cups of chicken stock to a boil. Drop dumpling mixture by rounded teaspoonfuls into boiling stock; simmer gently, uncovered, for 5 to 8 minutes or until well formed. Remove dumplings as they are finished and repeat process until all mixture is used. Set dumplings and their cooking stock aside to add to soup later. To make soup, in a large kettle, sauté the onions, celery and garlic in melted butter or margarine; stir in flour. Add 2 quarts chicken stock, stirring constantly; bring to a boil. Add salt and carrots; simmer, covered, for 15 minutes. Add dumplings, their cooking stock and cucumbers; simmer another 15 minutes. Makes 4 quarts.

AND A CATCH OF GREAT SEAFOOD SOUPS

SEAFOOD CHOWDER
here's how to delight a seafood lover

4 ounces salt pork, diced
1 cup chopped onions
2 cloves garlic, minced
1/2 cup chopped celery
3 cups cubed potatoes
2 (12 oz.) cans clam juice
1 teaspoon salt
1/4 teaspoon thyme
1/4 teaspoon paprika

2 teaspoons Worcestershire sauce
1-1/2 pounds boneless cod, haddock or halibut,
    cut into bite size pieces
1/2 pound cooked, shelled tiny shrimp
1/2 pound cooked lobster meat cut into
    bite-size pieces
1 quart (4 cups) milk
1/2 pint (1 cup) heavy cream
butter, for garnish

In a large kettle, cook salt pork until crisp and browned. Add onions, garlic and celery, and sauté until onions are transparent. Add potatoes, clam juice, salt, thyme, paprika and Worcestershire sauce. Bring to a boil, reduce heat and simmer, covered, for 10 minutes or until potatoes are only partially tender. Add fish and continue to simmer, covered, for 10 minutes or until fish flakes with a fork. Add shrimp, lobster meat, milk and cream. Reheat to serving temperature *but do not boil.* When serving, place pat of butter on each individual portion. Makes 3-1/2 quarts.

FILLET OF FISH SOUP
a colorful combination of fish and vegetables

3 tablespoons butter or margarine
1-1/2 cups chopped onions
3 cloves garlic, minced
1 cup sliced celery
1 (28 oz.) can tomatoes, chopped, and their
   liquid
1 (18 oz.) can tomato juice
1 quart (4 cups) basic chicken stock
  (see page 8)
2 teaspoons salt
1/2 teaspoon basil

1/4 teaspoon oregano
1 bay leaf
2 whole cloves
1 tablespoon Worcestershire sauce
1/2 cup white rice
2 cups fresh green beans, cut *or*
   1 (10 oz.) package frozen cut green beans
2/3 cup dry white wine
2 pounds fish fillets (cod, halibut, sea bass,
   turbot, etc.) cut into bite size pieces

In a large kettle, melt butter or margarine; sauté onions, garlic, and celery until onions are limp. Add tomatoes, their liquid, tomato juice, chicken stock, salt, basil, oregano, bay leaf, cloves and Worcestershire sauce; bring to a boil. Add rice and green beans; reduce heat and simmer, covered, for 30 minutes or until rice and beans are tender. Add wine and fish; continue to simmer 10 minutes or until fish flakes with a fork. Makes 4 quarts.

SALMON BISQUE
serve garnished with popcorn

1-1/2 cups chopped onions
2 cups cubed potatoes
2 cups sliced celery
1/2 cup chopped fresh parsley
1 (16 oz.) can tomato purée
1 quart (4 cups) water
1/2 cup dry white wine
2 teaspoons salt

1/4 teaspoon pepper
1/2 teaspoon thyme
1/4 teaspoon basil
1 (16 oz.) can salmon
1/4 cup butter or margarine
1/4 cup all-purpose flour
1 pint (2 cups) half and half (light cream)
popcorn, for garnish

In a large kettle, combine onions, potatoes, celery, parsley, tomato purée, water, wine, salt, pepper, thyme, basil and salmon. Bring to a boil, reduce heat and simmer, covered, for 30 minutes. In a saucepan, melt butter or margarine and blend in flour. Gradually add half and half. Cook, stirring constantly, until thickened and smooth. Stir thickened sauce into soup, mixing well. Reheat soup to serving temperature *but do not boil*. Garnish each serving with popcorn. Makes 3-1/2 quarts.

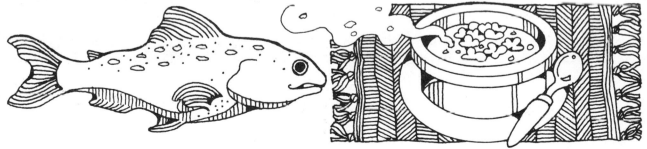

TUNA CHOWDER
garnish with chopped chives or green onion tops

2 cups chopped onions
1-1/2 cups sliced celery and leaves
1 cup firmly packed, shredded carrots
2 cups diced potatoes
1-1/2 quarts (6 cups) water
2 teaspoons salt
1/4 teaspoon pepper
1/4 teaspoon savory
1/3 cup butter or margarine
1/3 cup all-purpose flour
1 pint (2 cups) half and half (light cream)
3 cups shredded sharp cheddar cheese
1 (17 oz.) can cream style corn
2 (6-1/2 oz.) cans tuna, drained
chives or green onion tops, for garnish

In a large kettle, combine the onions, celery, carrots, potatoes, water, salt, pepper and savory; bring to a boil. Reduce heat and simmer, uncovered, for 15 minutes or until potatoes are tender. In a saucepan, melt butter or margarine; blend in flour. Gradually stir in the half and half; cook, stirring constantly, until smooth and thickened. Add cheese and stir until completely melted. Add cheese sauce and corn to cooked vegetables, stirring until smooth and well blended. Flake tuna into soup; reheat to serving temperature *but do not boil.* Garnish with chives or green onion. Makes 4 quarts.

CRAB GUMBO

serve this Creole dish with crusty bread and sweet butter

1/4 cup butter or margarine
1 cup chopped onions
1 cup chopped celery
2 cloves garlic, minced
1 large sweet red *or*
  green pepper, chopped
1/4 cup all-purpose flour
1-1/2 quarts (6 cups) basic beef stock
  (see page 7)
1 (28 oz.) can tomatoes, chopped, and their
  liquid
1/2 cup chopped parsley

1 bay leaf
1 teaspoon paprika
1/2 teaspoon thyme leaves
1 tablespoon Worcestershire sauce
1 teaspoon salt
1/4 teaspoon pepper
1 (10 oz.) package frozen succotash
1/2 pound fresh okra, sliced *or*
  frozen okra, sliced into 1/2-inch slices
1 pound crab meat
cooked, hot rice (1/2 cup per serving)
hot pepper sauce

In a large kettle, melt butter or margarine; sauté the onions, celery, garlic, and sweet pepper for 3 minutes. Sprinkle with flour and mix thoroughly. Gradually add beef stock; cook and stir until smooth. Add tomatoes, their liquid, parsley, bay leaf, paprika, thyme, Worcestershire sauce, salt, pepper and succotash. Bring to a boil; reduce heat and simmer, covered, for 30 minutes or until lima beans are tender. Add okra and crab meat and continue to simmer for 20 minutes. Put a scoop (1/2 cup) of cooked, hot rice into center of each individual bowl and fill bowl with gumbo. Let individuals add the hot pepper sauce to their taste. Makes 3-1/2 quarts.

CLAM BISQUE
pale pink and creamy, this soup deserves your finest china

1/2 cup butter or margarine
1-1/4 cups finely chopped onions
2 cloves garlic, finely minced
1/2 cup all-purpose flour
2 (12 oz.) cans clam juice
5 (6-1/2 oz.) cans minced clams
1 quart (4 cups) half and half (light cream)
1/4 cup tomato paste
1/4 cup fresh lemon juice
1 teaspoon salt

In a large kettle melt butter or margarine and sauté onions and garlic until transparent. Stir in flour; cook, stirring constantly, just until bubbly. Stir in clam juice and minced clams; cook, stirring constantly until mixture thickens and comes to a boil. Boil 1 minute; reduce heat, cover and simmer 20 to 25 minutes. Blend in half and half, tomato paste, lemon juice and salt. Heat very slowly over lowest heat until piping hot (takes about 30 minutes). Makes 3 quarts.

CLAM VEGETABLE SOUP
a great choice for a Saturday night

3 tablespoons butter or margarine
1 cup chopped onions
2 cloves garlic, minced
1/2 cup chopped celery
1/2 cup chopped carrots
1 medium size sweet green pepper, chopped
2 quarts (8 cups) basic chicken stock
  (see page 8)
1 (16 oz.) can tomatoes, chopped and their
  liquid
1/4 cup chopped fresh parsley

1-1/2 cups chopped cabbage
1-1/2 cups chopped potatoes
1 teaspoon salt
1/8 teaspoon crushed, dried red peppers
1/2 teaspoon rosemary leaves
1/2 teaspoon marjoram
1 (8-3/4 oz.) can red kidney beans, drained
  and liquid saved
1 (8-3/4 oz.) can garbanzo beans, drained
1/4 cup cornstarch
3 (6-1/2 oz.) cans minced clams, with liquid

In a large kettle, melt butter or margarine and sauté onions, garlic, celery, carrots and green pepper until onions are limp. Add chicken stock, tomatoes, their liquid, parsley, cabbage, potatoes, salt, red pepper, rosemary and marjoram. Bring to a boil, reduce heat and simmer, covered, for 30 minutes. Add drained kidney beans and garbanzo beans. In a small bowl, combine cornstarch and reserved kidney bean liquid. Gradually stir mixture into soup. Stir until soup thickens slightly. Add clams with clam liquid and cook until heated through. Makes 4 quarts.

AVOCADO SHRIMP SOUP
a delicately flavored party soup

2 quarts (8 cups) basic chicken stock
  (see page 8)
1 cup chopped onions
1 cup chopped celery
1/2 cup chopped fresh parsley
2 bay leaves
1/2 teaspoon mace
1 teaspoon salt
1/8 teaspoon pepper
3 medium, ripe avocados, peeled and chopped
1/2 pint (1 cup) plain yogurt
12 ounces cooked, shelled tiny shrimp

In a large kettle, combine the chicken stock, onions, celery, parsley, bay leaves, mace, salt and pepper. Bring to a boil, reduce heat and simmer, covered, for 30 minutes. Remove bay leaves and purée broth two or three cups at a time in an electric blender or food processor. Return broth to kettle. Place the avocados into blender or processor and purée while adding 2 cups broth. When very smooth, return to kettle and mix thoroughly into soup with a wire whisk. Add yogurt and shrimp; reheat very gently but *do not allow to boil.* Makes 3 quarts.

CHEESY SCALLOP CHOWDER
complement this with a light fruit salad and muffins

1/4 cup butter or margarine
1-1/2 cups thinly sliced green onions
1 cup thinly sliced celery
1/2 cup chopped fresh parsley
1/2 cup white rice
1-1/2 quarts (6 cups) basic chicken stock
  (see page 8)
1-1/2 teaspoons salt
1/8 teaspoon pepper

1/4 teaspoon mace
1/4 teaspoon savory
2 teaspoons Worcestershire sauce
1/4 cup all-purpose flour
1/2 cup dry white wine
1 pound scallops, cut into bite size pieces
1 pint (2 cups) half and half (light cream)
3 cups shredded mild cheddar cheese

In a large kettle, melt butter or margarine; sauté onions, celery, parsley and rice until onions are limp. Add the chicken stock, salt, pepper, mace, savory and Worcestershire sauce. Bring to a boil; reduce heat and simmer, covered, for 10 minutes or until rice is almost tender. In a small bowl mix flour into wine; stir into chowder until smooth and thickened. Add scallops and cook for 5 minutes. Add half and half and cheese; reheat slowly to serving temperature *but do not boil*. Makes 3 quarts.

RECIPE INDEX